THE CASE FOR

Heaven

[AND HELL]

—

A Journalist Investigates
Evidence for Life After Death

STUDY GUIDE | FIVE SESSIONS

LEE
STROBEL

WITH BILL BUTTERWORTH

Harper*Christian*
Resources

The Case for Heaven [and Hell] Study Guide
© 2021 by Lee Strobel

Requests for information should be addressed to:
HarperChristian Resources, 3900 Sparks Dr. SE, Grand Rapids, Michigan 49546

ISBN 978-0-310-13547-0 (softcover)
ISBN 978-0-310-13548-7 (ebook)

HarperChristian Resources titles may be purchased in bulk for church, business, fundraising, or ministry use. For information, please e-mail ResourceSpecialist@ChurchSource.com.

Cover designer: Curt Diepenhorst
Cover photo: Krystiannawrocki / Getty Images
Interior design: Sara Colley

Published in association with The Gates Group (the-gates-group.com)

Second Printing December 2021 / Printed in the United States of America

Contents

How to Use This Guide

Need some answers to questions about the afterlife, heaven, and hell? Then you are in the right place. *The Case for Heaven [and Hell]* is designed to be experienced in a group setting (such as a Bible study, Sunday school class, or any small group gathering) and also as an individual study.

Each session begins with a brief opening reflection and several icebreaker-type questions to get you and your group thinking about the topic. You will then watch a video with Lee Strobel, which can be accessed via the streaming code found on the inside front cover. If you are doing the study with a group, you will then engage in some directed discussion. You will close each session with a time of personal reflection and prayer.

Each person in the group should have his or her own study guide, which includes video teaching notes, Bible study and group discussion questions, and between-sessions personal studies to help you reflect on and apply the material to your life during the week. You are also encouraged to have a copy of *The Case for Heaven* book, as reading it alongside the curriculum will provide you with deeper insights and make the journey more meaningful.

To get the most out of your group experience, keep the following points in mind. First, the real growth in this study will happen during your small-group time. This is where you will process the content of Lee's message, ask questions, and learn from others as you hear what God is doing in their lives. For this reason, it is important for you to be fully committed to the group and attend each session so you can build trust and rapport with the other members. If you choose to only "go through the motions," or if you refrain from participating, there is a lesser chance you will find what you're looking for during this study.

Second, remember the goal of your small group is to serve as a place where people can share, learn about God, and build intimacy and friendship. For this reason, seek to make your group a "safe place." This means being honest about your thoughts and feelings and listening carefully to everyone else's opinion. Third, resist the temptation to "fix" someone's problem or correct his or her theology, as that's not the purpose of your small-group time. Also, keep everything your group shares confidential. This will foster a rewarding sense of community in your group and create a place where people can heal, be challenged, and grow spiritually.

In between your group times, you can maximize the impact of the course by checking out the personal study guide activities. This individual study will help you personally reflect and actively respond to the lesson. For each session, you may wish to complete the personal study in one sitting or spread it over a few days (for example, working on it a half-hour per day on four different days that week). Note that if you are unable to finish (or even start!) your between-sessions personal study, you should still attend the group study video session. You are still wanted and welcome at the group even if you don't have your "homework" done.

Keep in mind this study is an opportunity for you to train in a new way of seeing what heaven, hell, and the afterlife are all about. The videos, discussions, and activities are simply meant to kick-start your imagination, so you are open not only to what God wants you to hear but also to how to apply that message to your life.

Sound good? Well . . . then let's get started!

Can We Really Know There Is a Heaven?

. . . .

Just as people are destined to die once, and after that to face judgment so Christ was sacrificed once to take away the sins of many; and he will appear a second time, not to bear sin, but to bring salvation to those who are waiting for him.

Hebrews 9:27–28

Welcome

"Good people go to heaven. Bad people go to hell."

This is the theology one of my friends grew up with. "It never really bothered me," he told me, "until they added the tagline, 'By the way, you're a *bad person*.' With that information as a backdrop, you can see why heaven was always a frustrating and confusing topic for me.

"I used to dream about heaven every night," he continued. "Part of that was because my mother used to scold me for the way I was lying in bed. I would have my head on a pillow with another pillow over my head to block out any sights or sounds. 'Oh no, no, no!' she would warn dramatically. 'If you sleep like that, you could suffocate and *die* overnight!'

"So, of course, I would dream that I would die and immediately go stand before the Lord in front of the Pearly Gates. God would say hello and then explain how it all works.

"'We've got a giant scale up here,' he would tell me, pointing to one of those old-fashioned scales, complete with two platters. 'Some angels are going to put all your good works on one side and all your bad works on the other side. It's very simple, really. If your good works outweigh your bad works, *you're in*. But if your bad works outweigh your good works . . . well, the elevator is that way.' I wasn't real hopeful about how this was going to play out.

"'Bring in the good works,' I would hear the Lord announce. A rather anemic-looking angel soon appeared to bring my good works to the scale. I swallowed hard as I realized the good works had barely caused the scale to move.

"'Now bring in the bad works,' God said. His command was followed by the appearance of an angel who looked like a professional weightlifter, exclaiming at full voice, 'Okay, back 'er up, fellows!' as a tractor trailer began to unload tons of bad works. God pointed to the elevator. And that ended my glimpse of heaven."

What's your story? What were your earliest ideas of heaven? Or perhaps you were brought up to believe there was no heaven, because there was no afterlife. Once your days were over on this earth, you simply ceased to exist—or you came back as an armadillo or a golden retriever. We've all grown up with a variety of beliefs when it comes to heaven and hell.

Consider

Pair up with another group member, preferably someone you don't know that well, and briefly talk about the following questions:

- Do you remember the first time you really thought about heaven and an afterlife? What were your beliefs at that time?
- What are your current beliefs about heaven and an afterlife? How has your thinking changed over the years?

Watch

Play the video segment for session one (see the streaming video access provided on the inside front cover). As you watch, use the following outline to record any thoughts or concepts that stand out to you.

It's human nature for those who don't believe in God or an afterlife to want to be remembered by what they achieved while on this earth.

One of the most famous examples is the story of Herostratus, who in 356 BC burned down the Temple of Artemis in Ephesus. He stated the reason was because he wanted to be famous.

The bottom line is that if you don't have faith in God, you will likely find yourself with a desperate desire to cling to life in some way.

Another way that people try to achieve immortality without God is to figure out how to live longer in order to cheat death.

The answer to our dilemma can only be found in the Bible. In Hebrews 2:15, we find that Jesus came to rescue those who are "held in slavery by their fear of death."

Jesus uses the imagery of a home to convey the love, security, and comfort of the world where we will live after this one—what the Bible calls the new heavens and the new earth.

In Hebrews 10:23 we read, "Let us hold unswervingly to the hope we profess, for he who promised is faithful." God is ready, willing, and able to fulfill his promises to us.

God doesn't want us living in a state of anxiety over what will happen to us at the end of our lives. We can be confident about what will come next—and that it is going to be good.

Discuss

Once the video has concluded, it's time to break up into small groups for a time of discussion. Ideally, the group should be no less than four people and no more than six. Don't be shy—grab your chair and circle up! Find someone in your group that will become your partner over the next few weeks. If you're married and your spouse is in the group, you have the option of choosing him or her or you may opt for someone completely different. If not your spouse, it's best to for women to choose another woman and men to choose another man. Get your new partner's cell phone number and email—you two are going to be connecting during the week!

1. How old were you when you first came face to face with your mortality? What prompted you to wonder about what happens when your heart stops beating?

2. What are some of the events in your life (such as the death of a loved one) that have caused you to wonder about the afterlife? What questions did you have?

3. What are some of the ways that you have seen people try to leave a "mark" on this world so they will not be forgotten after they die?

4. What are some of the fears that you have heard people expresses about death?

5. **Read aloud John 3:16, John 5:24, Romans 6:23, and Galatians 6:8.** What do these verses say about the hope we can have that there is life after death?

6. Share with the group one or two questions you are hoping to be answered by your participation in this group. What did you find helpful as you watched the first video?

Respond

Briefly review the outline for the session one teaching and any notes you took. In the space below, write down your most significant takeaway from this session.

Pray

Conclude your group discussion time with a few minutes for prayer. Nothing will bring your group together quicker than knowing you have brothers and sisters who care enough about the issues you raise to bring them before the Lord for his answers and direction.

Between-Sessions Personal Study

Following each week's group time, you will be given the opportunity to reflect on the content you've covered by engaging in between-sessions personal studies. Before you begin this week, you may want to review the introduction and chapters 1–2 in *The Case for Heaven*. The time you invest in engaging in these personal studies will be well spent, so let God use it to draw you closer to him and give you hope concerning the afterlife. At your next meeting, share with your group any key points or insights that stood out to you as you spent this time with the Lord.

Study

Quite a few Scriptures were quoted in this session, so let's dig a little deeper into each of them. The seven verses from this session are printed on the next page. Using the chart on page 11, summarize in a phrase or sentence the main teaching of each verse, and then use the far-right column to write out an answer to the question: *What does it mean to me?* It's okay if you still have more questions about these verses. That's why we're in this study together!

> People are destined to die once, and after that to face judgment (Hebrews 9:27).

> He has made everything beautiful in its time. He has also set eternity in the human heart; yet no one can fathom what God has done from beginning to end (Ecclesiastes 3:11).

> He too shared in their humanity so that by his death he might break the power of him who holds the power of death—that is, the devil—and free those who all their lives were held in slavery by their fear of death (Hebrews 2:14–15).

> "My Father's house has many rooms; if that were not so, would I have told you that I am going there to prepare a place for you?" (John 14:2)

> However, as it is written: "What no eye has seen, what no ear has heard, and what no human mind has conceived"—the things God has prepared for those who love him (1 Corinthians 2:9).

> Let us hold unswervingly to the hope we profess, for he who promised is faithful (Hebrews 10:23).

> I write these things to you who believe in the name of the Son of God so that you may know that you have eternal life (1 John 5:13).

Passage	What It Says	What It Means to Me
Hebrews 9:27		
Ecclesiastes 3:11		
Hebrews 2:15		
John 14:2		
1 Corinthians 2:9		
Hebrews 10:23		
1 John 5:13		

Act

Take some time this week to think about how the material you are covering in this study can make a difference in the way that you lead your life. In the New Testament book of James, the author implores us to "not merely listen to the word" but also "do what it says" (1:22). The real test of what is important to us is how well we integrate it into our lives.

1. Based on what we've studied and discussed so far, finish the following sentences:

   When it comes to life after death, I believe . . .

   Regarding a place called heaven, I believe . . .

2. As you think about your family and friends, what do they believe concerning the afterlife? Do they believe like you or differently than you? Explain.

3. Consider some people in your life who have fears or doubts about the afterlife. What can you share with them this week to give them the hope you have found in Christ?

4. "Always be prepared to give an answer to everyone who asks you to give the reason for the hope that you have" (1 Peter 3:15). Why is it important to "always be prepared" when it comes to sharing your faith? What do you need to do to be better prepared?

Connect

Make contact with your new partner either through text or, better yet, a phone call. Check in to see how the person is doing. Is he or she enjoying the study? Are there any frustrations or confusions the person wants to verbalize? How do these truths about heaven and the afterlife make a difference in the way that person is living his or her life? Is there anything you can do to be of help to them between now and the next time the entire group gets together? Talk to your partner about the answers to the previous questions—big truths you've come away with as a result of the study and how the time together has made a change in your life.

Reflect

Interview with Dr. Sharon Dirckx

Each session will conclude with a portion of an interview from *The Case for Heaven*. The first interview is with Dr. Sharon Dirckx, a senior tutor at Oxford Centre for Christian Apologetics. She lectures internationally on science, theology, mind and soul issues, and other topics. She also appears regularly on British radio programs, sometimes debating secular thinkers.

"As a neuroscientist, I've measured the electrical activity of people's brains, but I can't measure their experience in the same way. I can't measure what's in their minds. I can't measure what it's actually like to be *you*. Why not? Because the brain alone is not enough to explain the mind."

To illustrate further, Dirckx described a thought experiment.[1] What if Mary were a scientist who had detailed knowledge of the physics and chemistry of vision? She knew all about the intricate structure of the eye, how it functions, and how it sends electrical signals to the brain through the optic nerve, where they're converted into images. But what if she was blind—and then one day suddenly she was able to see?

"At the moment of receiving her sight, does Mary learn anything new about vision?" Dirckx asked.

My eyes widened. "Of course!"

"That means physical facts alone cannot explain the first-person experience of consciousness. No amount of knowledge about the physical working of the eye and brain would get Mary closer to the experience of what it's like to actually *see*."

"What's your conclusion?"

"That consciousness simply cannot be synonymous with brain activity."

"You're saying that although they work together, they're not the same thing. Consciousness—the mind, the soul—are beyond the physical workings of the brain."

"Correct. Philosophers such as Leibniz make an important point: If two things are identical, there would be no discernible difference between them.[2] That means if consciousness were identical with brain activity, everything true of consciousness would be true of the brain as well. But consciousness and brain activity couldn't be more different. So consciousness cannot be reduced to the purely physical processes of the brain."

She pointed toward me and smiled. "You, Lee, are more than just your brain."

That did seem clear-cut—but there have been objections. "The atheist Daniel Dennett gets around this by saying that consciousness is illusory," I said.

She replied simply. "Illusion still presupposes consciousness."

"Could you explain that?"

"Illusion happens when we misinterpret an experience or perceive it wrongly, but the experience itself is still valid and real. So that's a problem with what he's saying. Honestly, I think his view is absurd. By the way, it backfires. If what he claims is true, then his very argument can't be trusted."

"Why not?"

"Because it's just an illusion."

Neuroscientist Adrian Owen spent more than two decades studying patients with brain trauma. In 2006, the prestigious journal *Science* published his groundbreaking research showing that some patients considered vegetative with severe brain injuries were actually conscious.

Said Owen, "We have discovered that 15 to 20 percent of people in the vegetative state, who are assumed to have no more awareness than a head of broccoli, are in fact fully conscious, even though they never respond to any form of external stimulation."[3]

"What does that tell you?" I asked Dirckx.

"It's additional evidence that human beings are highly complex, and the condition of our brains is only part of the story," she said. "Consciousness goes beyond our physical brain and nervous system. It can't just be boiled down to brain activity. *We* are more than our brains."

That triggered thoughts about experiments in the 1950s by Wilder Penfield, the father of modern neurosurgery, who stimulated the brains of epilepsy patients, creating all kinds of involuntary sensations and movements. But no matter how much he tried, he couldn't evoke abstract reasoning or consciousness itself.

"There is no place . . . where electrical stimulation will cause a patient to believe or to decide," Wilder said.[4] For him, this evidence for a nonphysical mind distinct from the brain convinced him to abandon physicalism.[5]

But could the brain, as it evolved in complexity, have somehow generated the conscious mind? I asked Dirckx about this view, which is popular among many scientists.

"If we're dealing with a closed system of nonconscious neurons, how did these come to generate conscious minds?" she replied, letting the challenge hang in the air for a few moments. "This has been the big hurdle. Nobody can give a coherent explanation for it in a materialist world. And if all that's needed is a physical brain to create the mind, why aren't animals conscious to the same degree as we are? The discontinuity between primates and people isn't one of *degree*; it's one of *kind*. Complexity, all by itself, wouldn't be enough to get us across that chasm. Of course, there are Christians who take an emergent view, but for them, the system is not closed. If God exists, extraordinary things are possible. Then that chasm can be crossed."

—*From chapter 2 of* The Case for Heaven

For Next Week: Before your group's next session, read chapters 3–4 in *The Case for Heaven.*

What's the Evidence for Heaven?

. . . .

"My Father's house has many rooms; if that were not so, would I have told you that I am going there to prepare a place for you? And if I go and prepare a place for you, I will come back and take you to be with me that you also may be where I am."

John 14:2–3

Welcome

Centenarians. The term sounds like a denominational branch of Christianity, like a Presbyterian or an Episcopalian. Or a person who collects cents . . . or centipedes. All kidding aside, the *Oxford Dictionary* defines a *centenarian* as a person who reaches 100 or more years in age. Those who reach more than 110 years in age are given the title of *supercentenarian.*

In the last session, we noted that one way people try to achieve immortality without God is to try to live longer and longer in order to cheat death. It looks like these centenarians are trying to figure that out! Many of the *supercentenarians* reach impressive ages indeed.

The oldest living person on record is Jeanne Calment of France, who reached the age of 122 years, 164 days, before her death in 1997. She is followed by Sarah Knauss of the United States, who reached 119 years, 97 days, before her death in 1999. The oldest living man is Jiroemon Kimua of Japan, who was 116 years, 54 days old before his death in 2013.[1]

Yet the statistics overall are against people ever becoming centenarians. According to one study, Japan is the country with the highest rate of centenarians, at 6 for every 10,000 people, or approximately 0.06 percent.[2] Not very encouraging . . . and Americans are way behind that statistic. According to another report, today only 0.0173 percent of Americans live to 100.[3] While some families have a disproportionate number of people who live to 100, in the general population, living to 100 continues to remain an unusual event.

The truth is that attempting to live longer in an attempt to "cheat" death is just an exercise in frustration. After all, even if you lived to the age of *200,* you would still not cheat death. As one writer put it, "Like water spilled on the ground, which cannot be recovered, so we must die" (2 Samuel 14:14). Death would be right there waiting for you . . . leading you into the afterlife that is eternal. And the afterlife will make 200 years look like a sneeze.

Now, don't get me wrong, there's nothing wrong with taking good care of yourself and trying to live a long and healthy life. On one hand, we salute all those centenarians out there for their unusual accomplishment. But rather than focus our attention on how to live longer on earth, it makes better sense for us to more fully understand the evidence for heaven!

Consider

Take some time to share at least one key takeaway or insight you had from last week's personal studies. Then, to get things started, pair up with another group member (preferably someone you don't know that well) and briefly talk about the following questions:

- Have you read any books or seen documentaries on near death experiences? If so, what was your impression of what you were reading or seeing?
- What evidence have you discovered for the existence of heaven? How do you respond to people who say that there is no such place?

Watch

Play the video segment for session two (see the streaming video access provided on the inside front cover). As you watch, use the following outline to record any thoughts or concepts that stand out to you.

Corroboration is important when we're trying to discern the truth. So, when the Bible teaches that people continue to live on forever in heaven or hell after their death, we need to determine if there is any evidence to corroborate this claim.

The Bible has excellent historical credentials. The four Gospels are rooted in direct and indirect eyewitness testimony, were written close to the events they describe, have been reliably preserved, and are corroborated in key points by archaeology and outside writings.

The evidence of neuroscience points toward us being both a body and a soul that is capable of surviving our bodies' death. The Bible presupposes that our souls are real.

Consciousness, our soul or spirit, is distinct from our physical body. The Bible says that humans were made in God's image (see Genesis 1:27). So, it makes sense that we have a consciousness just as God does. We have a soul separate from our body that could survive our death.

This can be corroborated by accounts of near-death experiences. In one study, a researcher studied 93 patients who made verifiable observations while out of their physical bodies. A remarkable 92 percent of these observations were completely accurate.

We also have the firsthand account of Jesus about the life beyond. His conquering of the grave is among the best attested events of the ancient world. There is no record anywhere of anyone else ever surviving a full Roman crucifixion. His death is indisputable.

In the words of Sir Lionel Luckhoo, the most successful defense attorney of all time, "The evidence for the resurrection of Jesus Christ is so overwhelming that it compels acceptance by proof which leaves absolutely no room for doubt."

All of this makes Jesus an actual eyewitness to the afterlife, not to mention proving that he is the Son of God, which means we can trust his account of what happens after we die.

Discuss

Once the video has concluded, break up into small groups for a time of discussion. Ideally, this should be the group with whom you've spent the previous session—and by now you should be growing more comfortable with one another. Circle up and get right down to it!

1. The term *corroborate* means to "support with evidence or authority." In criminal cases, why is it important to have corroboration from witnesses to determine the truth?

2. The four Gospels are rooted in direct and indirect eyewitness testimony, were written close to the events they describe, and have been reliably preserved throughout history. Why are these factors important to consider when judging whether the events about Jesus' life, ministry, death, and resurrection can be trusted to be accurate?

3. Near-death experiences can corroborate the Bible's claim that our soul continues to exist long after our physical death. Do you have any personal stories of a near-death experience involving someone you know? If so, share it with the group!

4. **Read aloud Genesis 1:27.** What does it mean that God created us in his image? What evidence does this provide that we have both a body and a soul?

5. What evidence do we have that Jesus actually died on a Roman cross?

6. What evidence do we have that Jesus was encountered alive after his death? Why is the death, burial, and resurrection of Jesus so important to our study of an afterlife?

Respond

Briefly review the outline for the session two teaching and any notes you took. In the space below, write down your most significant takeaway from this session.

Pray

Conclude your group discussion time with a few minutes for prayer. Nothing will bring your group together quicker than knowing you have brothers and sisters who care enough about the issues you raise to bring them before the Lord for his answers and his direction.

Between-Sessions Personal Study

Reflect on the content you've covered this week by engaging in any or all of the following between-sessions personal study. The time you invest will be well spent, so let God use it to draw you closer to him. At your next meeting, share with your group any key points or insights that stood out to you as you spent this time with the Lord.

Study

In this week's teaching, you examined several passages from the Bible which claim that after your physical death, you continue to live on forever in either a place called *heaven* or a place called *hell*. Let's dig down a little deeper into a few of the verses that were presented.

Part of studying the Bible on your own is discovering the answer to the question, *What is this portion of the Bible saying to me?* It is called *observation*, and it is the essential place to begin. Ultimately, you want to get to the point where you ask yourself, *What does this portion of the Bible mean to me?* With that question, you move from observation moved to *application*, where you are interacting with the verses on a more personal level.

An excellent method for achieving both *observation* and *application* is through the use of *paraphrasing.* This is where you write out the verses of the Bible in your own words. Paraphrasing forces you to interact with the text and creates a more personal connection with the verses. Today, read the following passages and then paraphrase in the table that follows.

> We are confident, I say, and would prefer to be away from the body and at home with the Lord (2 Corinthians 5:8).

> For what I received I passed on to you as of first importance: that Christ died for our sins according to the Scriptures, that he was buried, that he was raised on the third day according to the Scriptures, and that he appeared to Cephas, and then to the Twelve. After that, he appeared to more than five hundred of the brothers and sisters at the same time, most of whom are still living, though some have fallen asleep. Then he appeared to James, then to all the apostles, and last of all he appeared to me also, as to one abnormally born.
>
> For I am the least of the apostles and do not even deserve to be called an apostle, because I persecuted the church of God. But by the grace of God I am what I am, and his grace to me was not without effect. No, I worked harder than all of them—yet not I, but the grace of God that was with me. Whether, then, it is I or they, this is what we preach, and this is what you believed (1 Corinthians 15:3–11).

But if it is preached that Christ has been raised from the dead, how can some of you say that there is no resurrection of the dead? If there is no resurrection of the dead, then not even Christ has been raised. And if Christ has not been raised, our preaching is useless and so is your faith. More than that, we are then found to be false witnesses about God, for we have testified about God that he raised Christ from the dead. But he did not raise him if in fact the dead are not raised. For if the dead are not raised, then Christ has not been raised either. And if Christ has not been raised, your faith is futile; you are still in your sins. Then those also who have fallen asleep in Christ are lost. If only for this life we have hope in Christ, we are of all people most to be pitied (1 Corinthians 15:12–19).

"Very truly I tell you, whoever hears my word and believes him who sent me has eternal life and will not be judged but has crossed over from death to life" (John 5:24).

Passage	My Paraphrase
2 Corinthians 5:8	
1 Corinthians 15:1–11	
1 Corinthians 15:12–19	
John 5:24	

Now take a few minutes to respond to the following questions:

1. How did it feel to interact with the text in this way?

2. What do these passages teach you about the reality of an afterlife?

3. Why is the death and resurrection of Jesus important to this discussion?

4. What questions do you have that still remain unanswered regarding this topic?

Act

Recall Paul's words to the Corinthians: *"For what I received I passed on to you as of first importance: that Christ died for our sins according to the Scriptures, that he was buried, that he was raised on the third day according to the Scriptures"* (1 Corinthians 15:3–4). Paul was reminding the believers of the doctrine they had received regarding

Christ. But reflecting on this truth begs another question: *How often do we pause to thank Jesus for this sacrifice?*

For many of us, Jesus' death and resurrection are such common parts of our theology that we allow the significance of the events to pass us by. For this reason, today you will revisit the quaint custom of writing a *thank-you note.* Remember these when growing up? It was considered good manners to accept a gift and then follow it up with a handwritten note expressing your appreciation for the gift and the gift giver's thoughtfulness.

So, take some time today to say that well deserved "thank you" to the Lord. Use the prompts below to assist you in collecting your thoughts. Perhaps there are other things you would like to include in this letter to him—maybe some additional thoughts based on what you have learned in these first two sessions. If so, please feel free to include them!

Jesus, this comes to mind when I consider your sacrifice for me . . .

I want to tell you today that this is what your gift means to me . . .

I want the realization of your sacrifice to influence my actions in this way . . .

Most of all, I just want to say thank you for these things . . .

Connect

It's time to contact your partner once again, either by text or phone. Check in to see how he or she is doing. Is the person enjoying the study? Is there any frustration or confusion that the person can verbalize? What thoughts did the person have after doing the paraphrase and thank-you note exercises? How are the truths about heaven and the afterlife making a difference in the way he or she is living? Is there anything you can do to be of help between now and the next time the entire group gets together? Talk to your partner about the answers to the previous questions—big truths you've come away with as a result of the study and how the time together has made a change in your life.

Reflect

Interview with John Burke

John Burke is the founder of Gateway Church in Austin, Texas, and the author of *Imagine Heaven: Near-Death Experiences, God's Promises, and the Exhilarating Future That Awaits You*, which to date has sold nearly one million copies. Said philosopher J. P. Moreland, "In all honesty, this is now the go-to book on heaven and near-death experiences."[4]

"In all of your research," I asked, "what was your most surprising discovery about near-death experiences?"

"First, I'm not particularly fond of the term near-death experiences," he began. "As one survivor said, 'I wasn't *near* dead; I was *dead* dead.' Some of these cases involve people with no heartbeat or brain waves. There are instances where doctors had already declared them dead. They may not have been *eternally* dead, but many were certainly *clinically* dead."

"Okay, good point," I said.

"Now, let me answer your question," he continued. "What surprised me the most is that even though they vary a fair amount, these accounts have a common core—and incredibly, it's entirely consistent with what we're told about the afterlife in the Bible."

"Yet a lot of Christians associate NDEs with the occult or New Age thinking," I said.

"Not all Christians think that way. Many take the approach of the late theologian R. C. Sproul, who tried to keep an open mind about NDEs and encouraged more research and analysis.[5] Christian philosophers J. P. Moreland and Gary Habermas have been writing about the implications of NDEs as far back as the early 1990s."[6]

"Why is there such a wide variation in how people describe their NDE?"

"Well, I noticed that there's a difference between what people *report* they experienced and how they *interpret* it," he said. "The interpretations vary, but when you dig down to what they actually experienced, there's a core that's consistent with what Scripture tells us about the life to come."

I cocked my head. "As a pastor, you're not basing your theology about heaven on these NDEs, are you?" I asked.

"Not at all. I'm basing my beliefs on the Bible. That's our most reliable source. I'm merely saying that the Bible contains black-and-white words about the afterlife, and these NDEs tend to add color to the picture. They don't contradict; they complement."

"What do NDEs hold in common?" I asked.

"Three-quarters of people experience the separation of consciousness from the physical body," he replied.

"An out-of-body experience."

"That's right. About the same number have heightened senses and intense emotions."

"Positive ones?"

"Generally, yes. Two out of three encounter a mystical or brilliant light, and more than half meet other beings, either mystical ones or deceased relatives or friends. More than half describe unworldly or heavenly realms. A quarter say they undergo a life review. A third say they encounter a barrier or boundary, and more than half were aware of a decision to return to their physical body."

"Isn't it true that many people find it difficult to describe the experience?"

"For sure," he said. "A girl named Crystal said, 'There are no human words that even come close.' A guy named Gary said nothing could adequately describe the divine presence he encountered."[7]

"Tell me about that so-called divine presence," I said. "What do people typically say about him?"

"They talk about a brilliant light—brighter than anything they've ever seen," Burke said.

Then he told the story of an atheist named Ian McCormack from New Zealand, who went scuba diving off the coast of

Mauritius in the Indian Ocean and was stung four times by box jellyfish.

I cringed when he said that. I knew from my travels that these jellyfish are often called the world's most venomous creature. One sting can result in cardiovascular collapse and death in two to five minutes.[8] And Ian was stung *four* times.

"Ian was dying," Burke said. "He saw visions of his mother, who had told him to call out to God if he ever needed help. He was in utter darkness and felt terrified. He prayed for God to forgive his sins—and a bright light shined on him and literally drew him out of the darkness. He described the light as 'unspeakably bright, as if it was the center of the universe . . . more brilliant than the sun, more radiant than any diamond, brighter than a laser beam. Yet you could look right into it.'

"He said this presence knew everything about him, which made him feel terribly ashamed. But instead of judgment, he felt 'pure, unadulterated, clean, uninhibited, undeserved love.' He began weeping uncontrollably. Ian asked if he could 'step into the light.' As he did, he saw in the middle of the light a man with dazzling white robes—garments literally woven from light—who offered his arms to welcome him. He said, 'I knew that I was standing in the presence of Almighty God.'"[9]

Burke paused and then continued. "Remember the transfiguration? In Matthew 17:2, it says Jesus' face 'shone like the sun, and his clothes became as white as the light.'" He smiled. "Reminds me of that."

"But if Ian had been a Hindu, might he have encountered a god from that faith?"

"In all my research, I've never read of people describing anything like Krishna, who has blue skin, or Shiva, who has three eyes, or descriptions of the dissolving of the individual self in the impersonal supreme Brahma, which is the ultimate Hindu reality. In fact, two researchers studied five hundred Americans and five hundred Indians to see how much their cultural conditioning may have affected their NDE."

"What did they find?"

"That several basic Hindu ideas of the afterlife were never portrayed in the visions of the Indian patients. No reincarnation. They did describe encountering a white-robed man with a book of accounts. To them, that might vaguely suggest Karma, or the record of merits and demerits. But again, that's an interpretation, because it's also very consistent with what we find in the Bible."

—*From chapter 3 of* The Case for Heaven

For Next Week: Before your group's next session, read chapters 5–6 in *The Case for Heaven*.

What Will Heaven Be Like?

· · · · · · · ·

No longer will there be any curse. The throne of God and of the Lamb will be in the city, and his servants will serve him. They will see his face, and his name will be on their foreheads. There will be no more night. They will not need the light of a lamp or the light of the sun, for the Lord God will give them light. And they will reign for ever and ever.

Revelation 22:3–5

Welcome

Heaven is a popular topic in Hollywood, and there is probably no more imaginative movie about the afterlife than the romantic comedy *Defending Your Life*. First released in 1991, it stars Meryl Streep, Albert Brooks, and Rip Torn, all three in hilarious roles. On the positive side, it is a funny, clever, and well-acted film. But on the negative side, it is about as far away from the biblical teachings regarding heaven that one could imagine.

First of all, according to the movie, when you die you don't go directly to heaven or hell. Instead, you go to a place called Judgment City. There, your life is reviewed in a courtroom sort of environment. Video clips of your life are replayed in front of a judge, who is both stern and unbending. There is obviously a lot of stress.

Second, you are doing exactly what the title of the movie says—*defending your own life*. The movie has no reference to Jesus, his death on the cross, or the substitutionary atonement that he made for sin. You are just on your own. Much of the movie's humor is found in Albert Brooks' character, a pathetic and blundering sort of man, essentially pleading for mercy.

Finally, according to the movie, your destination in the afterlife depends entirely on your own human effort. This is so different from the Bible's message that "it is by grace you have been saved . . . it is the gift of God" (Ephesians 2:8). In the movie, if you have faced your fears on earth, you're in. But if you lived plagued by your fears, you are sent back to earth to do it all over again. Yep—through reincarnation, which is also *not* taught in the Bible.

So, if *Defending Your Life* got it all wrong, what is the truth? What will heaven truly be like? In this session, rather than taking our cues from Hollywood, we will actually see what the Bible has to say in answer to that question.

Consider

Take some time to share at least one key takeaway or insight you had from last week's personal studies. Then, to get things started, pair up with another group member and briefly talk about the following questions:

- Do you have a favorite book, movie, or TV show about heaven? Why is it your favorite?
- When you think of heaven, do you see pearly gates, streets of gold, and beautiful mansions? What are your images of heaven?

Watch

Play the video segment for session three (see the streaming video access provided on the inside front cover). As you watch, use the following outline to record any thoughts or concepts that stand out to you.

It is important to clarify there are two kinds of "heavens" where followers of Jesus will go after death. The first is the *intermediate state*. Our soul separates from our body and enters this so-called present heaven, where our spirit is conscious and aware of our situation.

The final judgment marks the onset of the *eternal state* of our existence—our forever life in heaven. Upon Jesus' triumphant return to earth, followers of Christ in the intermediate state will receive their imperishable resurrected body and graduate into the eternal heaven.

God will remake our current world into a transformed place for transformed people. In a similar way, we won't have new bodies in heaven. Instead, our current bodies will be made new.

The greatest experience of heaven will be seeing God face to face. In our fallen world, our finite and sinful bodies would simply collapse at the sight of him. But in paradise, in our resurrected bodies that cannot die, we will gaze upon the Lord himself.

Heaven will be a place of worship, but it will also be a place of relationships! There will be community and social engagement in heaven. It will be a glorious union of delight in God and delight in one another.

God will continually be creating a world of joy and wonder for us. After all, if he can create all the beauty of our current universe, he is certainly capable of creating an eternally stimulating and rewarding experience for his followers in the new heaven and new earth.

Heaven will be a place of healing, where the infirmities and disabilities of our present world will disappear. "There will be no more death or mourning or crying or pain" (Revelation 21:4).

Here's a question for you. Who would you like to meet in heaven? Who would you like to sit down with on your veranda and chat for hours?

Discuss

Once the video has concluded, break up into small groups for a time of discussion. Ideally, this should be the group with whom you've spent the previous session—and by now you should be growing more comfortable with one another. Circle up and get right down to it!

1. What are some of the ways that you have heard others describe heaven? How well do those depictions match up to what you read in the Bible?

2. What are you most looking forward to doing in heaven? Who are you most interested in seeing in that place? Explain.

3. What are the two kinds of "heavens" described in the Bible? How would you describe the difference between the intermediate and the eternal states?

4. What comes to mind when you consider that you will be seeing God face to face in heaven? Is it exciting? Scary? Hard to imagine? Explain.

5. Heaven will be a place of healing, where the infirmities and disabilities of our present world will disappear. What comes to mind when you picture how that will look?

6. **Read out loud 1 Corinthians 2:9 and Revelation 7:16–17.** Sit quietly for a few moments, and then reflect on these verses.

What stands out the most to you in these words from Scripture that you just read? Explain.

Respond

Briefly review the outline for the session three teaching and any notes you took. In the space below, write down your most significant takeaway from this session.

Pray

Conclude your group discussion time with a few minutes for prayer. Start by having everyone share how they are doing in regard to the issues you have been praying about this past week, and then continue to pray for those needs. Share any new requests that you would like the group members to pray about during the week ahead.

Between-Sessions
Personal Study

Reflect on the content you have covered this week by engaging in any or all of the following between-sessions personal study. The time you invest will be well spent, so let God use it to draw you closer to him. At your next meeting, share with your group any key points or insights that stood out to you as you spent time with the Lord.

Study

Perhaps the central passage in Scripture that best answers the question of what heaven will be like is found in the twenty-first chapter of the book of Revelation. Today, you will be carefully reading these twenty-seven verses and then using the chart that follows to record what each tells you about heaven. Most likely you will have more than one answer for each individual verse—and that's okay. The more detailed you can be, the better.

Then I saw "a new heaven and a new earth," for the first heaven and the first earth had passed away, and there was no longer any sea. I saw the Holy City, the new Jerusalem, coming down out of heaven from God, prepared as a bride beautifully dressed for her husband. And I heard a loud voice from the throne saying, "Look! God's dwelling place is now among the people, and he will dwell with them. They will be his people, and God himself will be with them and be their God. 'He will wipe every tear from their eyes. There will be no more death' or mourning or crying or pain, for the old order of things has passed away."

He who was seated on the throne said, "I am making everything new!" Then he said, "Write this down, for these words are trustworthy and true."

He said to me: "It is done. I am the Alpha and the Omega, the Beginning and the End. To the thirsty I will give water without cost from the spring of the water of life. Those who are victorious will inherit all this, and I will be their God and they will be my children. But the cowardly, the unbelieving, the vile, the murderers, the sexually immoral, those who practice magic arts, the idolaters and all liars—they will be consigned to the fiery lake of burning sulfur. This is the second death."

One of the seven angels who had the seven bowls full of the seven last plagues came and said to me, "Come, I will show you the bride, the wife of the Lamb." And he carried me away in the Spirit to a mountain great and high, and showed me the Holy City, Jerusalem, coming down out of heaven from God. It shone with the glory of God, and its brilliance was like that of a very precious jewel, like a jasper, clear as crystal. It had a great, high wall with twelve gates, and with twelve angels at the gates.

On the gates were written the names of the twelve tribes of Israel. There were three gates on the east, three on the north, three on the south and three on the west. The wall of the city had twelve foundations, and on them were the names of the twelve apostles of the Lamb.

The angel who talked with me had a measuring rod of gold to measure the city, its gates and its walls. The city was laid out like a square, as long as it was wide. He measured the city with the rod and found it to be 12,000 stadia in length, and as wide and high as it is long. The angel measured the wall using human measurement, and it was 144 cubits thick. The wall was made of jasper, and the city of pure gold, as pure as glass. The foundations of the city walls were decorated with every kind of precious stone. The first foundation was jasper, the second sapphire, the third agate, the fourth emerald, the fifth onyx, the sixth ruby, the seventh chrysolite, the eighth beryl, the ninth topaz, the tenth turquoise, the eleventh jacinth, and the twelfth amethyst. The twelve gates were twelve pearls, each gate made of a single pearl. The great street of the city was of gold, as pure as transparent glass.

I did not see a temple in the city, because the Lord God Almighty and the Lamb are its temple. The city does not need the sun or the moon to shine on it, for the glory of God gives it light, and the Lamb is its lamp. The nations will walk by its light, and the kings of the earth will bring their splendor into it. On no day will its gates ever be shut, for there will be no night there. The glory and honor of the nations will be brought into it. Nothing impure will ever enter it, nor will anyone who does what is shameful or deceitful, but only those whose names are written in the Lamb's book of life.

Verse	What It Teaches Me About Heaven
Verse 1	
Verse 2	
Verse 3	
Verse 4	
Verse 5	
Verse 6	
Verse 7	
Verse 8	
Verse 9	
Verse 10	

Verse	What It Teaches Me About Heaven
Verse 11	
Verse 12	
Verse 13	
Verse 14	
Verse 15	
Verse 16	
Verse 17	
Verse 18	
Verse 19	
Verse 20	

Verse	What It Teaches Me About Heaven
Verse 21	
Verse 22	
Verse 23	
Verse 24	
Verse 25	
Verse 26	
Verse 27	

Now let's dig a little deeper. Read the following words from noted Bible teacher Charles Swindoll, who offers a brief word study of the term *new*, as found in Revelation 21.

> The new heaven and new earth will be new not merely in a chronological sense, as we might talk about a "new day," for example. Rather, John describes qualitative newness (see Revelation 21:1). To use a film metaphor, this isn't a sequel—it's

a completely new and different production. It isn't simply a reedited version, enhanced with clearer sound, brighter colors and a smattering of digitally enhanced special effects. This is no reedit—it's a remake!

The Greek word *kainos*, "new," means "different from the usual, impressive, better than the old, superior in value or attraction." John had watched as the first heaven and earth "fled away" (verse 11), along with all the other associated contaminations of sin. In the next vision, John saw heaven and earth return—but this time a new heaven and a new earth, uncontaminated and unaffected by sin (see verse 1). Created by a perfect God who does perfect work, these will be perfect places existing in a perfect environment. One of today's Christian composers puts it well: "I can only imagine."[1]

1. "This is no reedit, it's a remake!" What does that mean to you?

2. What is the significance that the new heaven and earth is not tainted by sin?

Act

It's time to apply what you learned in this lesson. Much of what you can put into practice is a direct result of what is happening currently in your life. Perhaps you have recently lost a family member or close friend. Or, if not, you can certainly recall the loss of someone close to you in the past. Your loss has left a void—yet you know that person is now in heaven.

1. Based on what you learned in this session, what does it mean to you that your loved one is now in heaven with Christ?

2. What does it mean to you that one day *you* will be in heaven?

3. What is it about heaven that most excites you?

4. Who would be the top five people you want to visit with in heaven? Why those five?

Connect

It's time to contact your partner once again, either by text or phone call. Check in to see how he or she is doing. What is the person most looking forward to about heaven? Who does he or she want to meet in heaven? Is there any frustration or confusion the person wishes to verbalize? How do these truths about heaven and the afterlife make a difference in the way he or she is living? Is there anything you can do to be of help between now and the next time the entire group gets together? Talk to your partner about the answers to the previous questions—the big truths you have come away with as a result of the study and how the time together has made a change in your life.

Reflect

Interview with Dr. Scot McKnight

Dr. Scot McKnight is a highly influential and prolific New Testament scholar, with particular expertise in historical Jesus studies, the Gospels, early Christianity, and contemporary issues involving the church. Having grown up as the son of a Baptist deacon in Freeport, Illinois, he came to faith in Christ as a youngster and later had a transformative experience with the Holy Spirit at a church camp. He earned his master's degree from Trinity Evangelical Divinity School near Chicago and his doctorate from the University of Nottingham in England.

> "First," said McKnight, "I believe in heaven because Jesus and the apostles did. Jesus said, 'For my Father's will is that everyone who looks to the Son and believes in him shall have eternal life, and I will raise them up at the last day.' Peter promised his churches they would 'receive a rich welcome into the eternal kingdom of our Lord and Savior Jesus Christ.' As for John, he said, 'And this is what [God] promised us—eternal life.' Paul talked about our frail bodies, saying, 'For we know that if the earthly tent we live in is destroyed, we have a building from God, an eternal house

in heaven, not built by human hands' (see 2 Corinthians 5:1). If all of them believed in heaven, then it's good enough for me."

"What's your second reason?" I asked.

"Because Jesus was raised from the dead—to me, that's the big one," he replied. "Not only was he resurrected, but people saw his body; they talked with him; they ate with him; and then he returned to the Father with the promise that he will come back to consummate history. This gives great credibility to an afterlife—and as N. T. Wright said, 'The resurrection of Jesus is the *launching of God's new world.*'[2]

"My third reason for believing in heaven is that the overall Bible believes in it."

"Wait a second," I said. "The agnostic scholar Bart Ehrman says the earliest biblical books don't teach anything about heaven, and he seems to suggest that the concepts of heaven and hell were simply made up over the centuries."[3]

"Well, let's look at some facts," responded McKnight. "It's true that there's very little interest in heaven or the afterlife in the Old Testament. It speaks of death—or *sheol*—the way that other Near Eastern and Mediterranean cultures did at the time, which is that death seems to be permanent. *Sheol* is a dark, deep, and miry pit. In fact, the Old Testament's only statements about the afterlife are found in its latest books.[4] It's the New Testament that ushers in a new hope for eternal life and heaven."

"Should that bother Christians?" I asked.

"Not in the slightest, because this is how divine revelation works. It unfolds over time," he explained. "The Bible's major themes develop and grow and expand and take us to the very precipice of eternity. It's like watching a play, where the whole story isn't clear until the end. Once we get to Jesus, and especially his resurrection, the Old Testament's images of *sheol* give way to his glorious teachings of immortality, eternal life, and the kingdom of God."

"What's your fourth reason for believing in heaven?" I asked McKnight.

"Because the church has taught it consistently," he said.

I knew this was significant, because if the church had ever wavered on its teachings about eternal life or significantly altered them, this might indicate that the relevant biblical passages are ambiguous and can be legitimately interpreted in a variety of different ways.

"Christian theology from the very beginning has believed in an afterlife, especially because of the resurrection," McKnight told me. "There has never been an era in which the church hasn't believed in heaven.

"Then there's my fifth reason for believing in heaven—because of beauty."

That sounded intriguing. "How so?"

"Even atheists get awestruck by the grandeur of the world—visiting the Grand Canyon, strolling among the California redwoods, hearing Bach, or seeing a painting by Van Gogh. These point us toward something beyond. You see, many of us believe in heaven because we see in the present world a glimpse of something far grander—the world as we think it *ought* to be. Where do we get that sense of *ought*? Could it indicate a future reality—a new heaven and a new earth? If God made a world this good, doesn't it make sense he would make a world where it will all be even better?"

McKnight let that question linger for a minute. Then he moved on to his next reason for believing in heaven—namely, because most people do. He cited statistics showing that

84 percent of Americans believe in some kind of heaven, with nearly seven out of ten convinced that it's "absolutely true."[5]

Indeed, Todd Billings points out that even a third of those who *don't* believe in God *still* believe in life after death. In fact, he said, "belief in the afterlife appears to be on the rise" over recent years in America.[6] Said Jean Twenge, a researcher at San Diego State University, "It was interesting that fewer people participated in religion or prayed but more believed in an afterlife."[7]

McKnight told me, "Essentially, humans down through history and across the spectrum of religions and philosophies have always believed in an afterlife. Why is that? Is there something inherent in humans, a kind of innate intuition from God, that there's life beyond the grave? The Bible says God has 'set eternity in the human heart' (Ecclesiastes 3:11). I believe the history of human belief in heaven is an argument for believing it's true."

"What's your seventh reason?"

"Because of desire," he replied. "C. S. Lewis said, 'If we are made for heaven, the desire for our proper place will be already in us.' He said this is a desire that 'no natural happiness will satisfy.'[8] Elsewhere he explained, 'If I find in myself a desire which no experience in this world can satisfy, the most probable explanation is that I was made for another world.'[9] As philosopher Jerry Walls put it, 'A good God would not create us with the kind of aspirations we have and then leave those aspirations unsatisfied.'[10]

"I believe that the ongoing lack of fulfillment in possessing what we desire—the love of another, family, beauty, work—indicates there is a true home that will ultimately satisfy all our desires fully—and that home is heaven. In other words, the fleeting satisfactions of this world point beyond us toward a place of final and lasting fulfillment."

With that, McKnight went on to his eighth reason for believing in heaven—the desire for justice to be done.

"This world reeks of injustice. We've been told since childhood that life isn't fair." He gestured in the direction of the city of Chicago. "Not far from here, innocent kids in the inner city are getting shot. Sexual abuse and exploitation flourish around the world. When I was in high school, I thought racial discrimination would end in my generation, but it obviously didn't. We seem to have an innate sense of what's right and wrong, and we long to see justice done.

"I believe in heaven because I believe God wants to make all things right. He wants justice to be finally and fully established. That means victims of injustice will someday sit under the shade tree of justice and know that God makes all things so new that past injustices are swallowed up in the joy of the new creation."

"And what's your final reason?"

"Because science doesn't provide all the answers. We have an empirical mindset today. A lot of people believe scientific knowledge is superior to any other form of knowledge. But that's simply not true. Science can tell us how the world works and behaves, but it can't probe meaning and purpose. It can map brain function, but it can't explain love."

I interrupted to observe, "Even the statement that 'science is the only form of knowledge' is self-refuting, because that statement itself can't be confirmed by the scientific method."

"Right," he said. "The point is that science can't prove heaven, but not everything has to be subjected to scientific scrutiny. For instance, we have excellent historical evidence for Jesus' resurrection, and that ought to be sufficient to point toward the reality of an afterlife with God."

—*From chapter 5 of* The Case for Heaven

For Next Week: Before your group's next session, read chapters 7–8 in *The Case for Heaven*.

Is There Really a Place Called Hell?

. . . .

"He will reply, 'Truly I tell you, whatever you did not do for one of the least of these, you did not do for me.' Then they will go away to eternal punishment, but the righteous to eternal life."

Matthew 25:45–46

Welcome

At first glance, he looks like a human, complete with a pencil-thin mustache and well-manicured goatee that grows downward to a perfect razor-sharp point. But he has a pair of horns on his head and a long tail. Also, he is dressed completely in red . . . almost like he is wearing a pair of bright red long johns. He carries a pitchfork in a menacing manner. The only sound he makes is an evil laugh—just like the ones used by your favorite villain.

It's a good bet that you had this mysterious individual identified in about two seconds. We are talking about the devil. Lucifer. The evil one. The fallen angel also known as Satan.

We all know where Satan lives. In hell, of course. It is a place that most of us envision as just one big never-ending fire. Flames dance all around the devil that are wide enough to give the look of a "lake" of fire. The devil seems to float effortlessly over the flames, watching the fires inflict pain on the suffering inhabitants of the place.

If your vision of hell goes beyond the red-suited man, perhaps you see two large groups of people there. One group looks a lot like the devil. These are his demons—the ones who do his additional dirty work. The other group breaks your heart to look upon them. It's a group of humans, like you and me, their bodies on fire, burning up, but never completely consumed.

It will come as no surprise that none of those descriptions, either of Satan or hell, are accurate according to the Bible. Somehow, through the annals of time, well-meaning people have created these images that have permeated our thinking for hundreds of years.

However, while none of these particular depictions of Satan or hell are found in Scripture, it is not to say the Bible is silent on the subject. In one notable instance, Jesus gave the following warning to his disciples: "Do not be afraid of those who kill the body but cannot kill the soul. Rather, be afraid of the One who can destroy both soul and body in hell" (Matthew 10:28). The Greek word translated *hell* in this verse is *Gehenna*, a physical location outside the walls of Jerusalem where garbage was burned and where lepers and outcasts were sent.

In today's study, we will do a more careful examination about what God's Word has to say to us regarding this all-important subject. So, are you ready? Here we go.

Consider

- As you were growing up, what were you taught to believe about the devil? What were you taught to believe about the existence of a place called hell?
- Has your thinking changed over the years as you've grown and matured? If so, what are the differences from then till now?

Watch

Play the video segment for session four (see the streaming video access provided on the inside front cover). As you watch, use the following outline to record any thoughts or concepts that stand out to you.

The Bible teaches that a very real place called hell exists. But the specifics are open to controversy. As one author put it, the Bible is less clear on the nature of hell than on the existence of hell.

C. S. Lewis said hell was the one doctrine he wished he could discard. But he could not because: (1) it has the full support of Scripture, especially the Lord's own words; (2) it has always been held by Christendom; and (3) it has the support of reason.

Paul Copan notes that the two key images of hell—flames and darkness—represent existence away from the Lord's presence. This is the real essence of hell: being cut off from the source of life and joy and being separated from God's blessings forever.

God does not send people to hell. *People* send themselves to hell by separating themselves from the Lord. God simply speaks that sentence that they have passed upon themselves.

In Genesis 18:25 we read, "Will not the Judge of all the earth do *right?*" God will certainly do right. He will be fair in meting out his justice. So, the degree of suffering in eternity will be correlated to the degree of responsibility—which supports the reasonableness of the doctrine of hell.

Annihilationists and conditionalists believe the unredeemed simply cease to exist when they die—or they are resurrected for the final judgment and then consigned to hell for a limited period of punishment after which their lives are extinguished forever. Either way, there's no everlasting torment, because the unredeemed are snuffed out of existence.

Universalists propose another escape hatch by saying that in the end, God will forgive and adopt all people through Christ, perhaps after a limited period of restorative judgment in hell. This is an aberrant and dangerous doctrine that is flatly contradicted by Scripture.

Fortunately, while hell is a hard truth, it's not the only truth in the Bible. Jesus says he is the truth—and that he can and will provide the way to heaven for those who trust in him.

Discuss

Once the video has concluded, break up into small groups for a time of discussion. Ideally, this should be the group with whom you've spent the previous three sessions—and by now you should be more comfortable with one another. Circle up and go for it!

1. What are some common reasons why people are uncomfortable with the concept of hell? What has been your level of unease as you watched the teaching?

2. If the two key images of hell—flames and darkness—were taken literally, they would cancel each other out, because the flames would illuminate everything. So, how are we to understand these descriptions in the Bible as they relate to hell?

3. **Read aloud 2 Peter 3:9.** Why is it inaccurate to state that God sends people to hell? What is God actually doing for those who choose to reject his gift of salvation?

4. **Read aloud Matthew 11:21–22 and Luke 12:47–48.** How do these passages refute the idea that hell is "one size fits all" for all people?

5. **Read aloud Titus 2:11.** Supporters of universalism—that God will ultimately forgive and adopt all people through Christ— often cite this verse in support of their claim. But what does this verse say that God has actually done? What is our part in being saved?

6. Jesus said, "I am the way and the truth and the life. No one comes to the Father except through me" (John 14:6). What hope should this statement provide for each of us?

Respond

Briefly review the outline for the session four teaching and any notes you took. In the space below, write down your most significant takeaway from this session.

Pray

Take some time to pair up with your partner. How is he or she doing with this study? Does your partner have more questions than when you began? What are some ways you could help? Close by praying together as a group. Be sure to inquire about any new requests that might have surfaced since last session and continue to pray for the needs already before you.

Between-Sessions Personal Study

Reflect on the content you have covered this week by engaging in any or all of the following between-sessions personal study. The time you invest will be well spent, so let God use it to draw you closer to him. At your next meeting, share with your group any key points or insights that stood out to you as you spent time with the Lord.

Study

One way to look deeper into the meanings of words in Scripture is by reading them in a few different translations. Today, with the availability of translations on the internet, it's easier than ever to read the Bible in many different versions. The following verses covered in this week's teaching are printed in the New International Version. Read each passage on pages 68–70 and, in the table that follows, write down what it teaches you. Then choose your favorite two passages from the list and repeat the process but with different translations other than the NIV. (If two versions are too overwhelming, just do it with one other version. In the same vein, if you're really on a roll, don't stop at two—keep going!)

> Say to them, "As surely as I live, declares the Sovereign LORD, I take no pleasure in the death of the wicked, but rather that they turn from their ways and live. Turn! Turn from your evil ways! Why will you die, people of Israel?" (Ezekiel 33:11)

> "But I tell you, it will be more bearable for Tyre and Sidon on the day of judgment than for you. And you, Capernaum, will you be lifted to the heavens? No, you will go down to Hades. For if the miracles that were performed in you had been performed in Sodom, it would have remained to this day. But I tell you that it will be more bearable for Sodom on the day of judgment than for you" (Matthew 11:22–24).

> "The servant who knows the master's will and does not get ready or does not do what the master wants will be beaten with many blows. But the one who does not know and does things deserving punishment will be beaten with few blows. From everyone who has been given much, much will be demanded; and from the one who has been entrusted with much, much more will be asked" (Luke 12:47–48).

> "Far be it from you to do such a thing—to kill the righteous with the wicked, treating the righteous and the wicked alike. Far be it from you! Will not the Judge of all the earth do right?" (Genesis 18:25)

Multitudes who sleep in the dust of the earth will awake: some to everlasting life, others to shame and everlasting contempt (Daniel 12:2).

"Then he will say to those on his left, 'Depart from me, you who are cursed, into the eternal fire prepared for the devil and his angels....' Then they will go away to eternal punishment, but the righteous to eternal life" (Matthew 25:41, 46).

They will be punished with everlasting destruction and shut out from the presence of the Lord and from the glory of his might on the day he comes to be glorified in his holy people and to be marveled at among all those who have believed. This includes you, because you believed our testimony to you (2 Thessalonians 1:9–10).

After that, we who are still alive and are left will be caught up together with them in the clouds to meet the Lord in the air. And so we will be with the Lord forever (1 Thessalonians 4:17).

For the grace of God has appeared that offers salvation to all people (Titus 2:11).

The Lord is not slow in keeping his promise, as some understand slowness. Instead he is patient with you, not wanting anyone to perish, but everyone to come to repentance (2 Peter 3:9).

For God so loved the world that he gave his one and only Son, that whoever believes in him shall not perish but have eternal life (John 3:16).

All inhabitants of the earth will worship the beast—all whose names have not been written in the Lamb's book of life, the Lamb who was slain from the creation of the world (Revelation 13:8).

For I could wish that I myself were cursed and cut off from Christ for the sake of my people, those of my own race (Romans 9:3).

"Make every effort to enter through the narrow door, because many, I tell you, will try to enter and will not be able to" (Luke 13:24).

Verse(s)	What This Passage Reveals to Me
Ezekiel 33:11	
Matthew 11:22–24	
Luke 12:47–48	
Genesis 18:25	
Daniel 12:2	
Matthew 25:41, 46	
2 Thessalonians 1:9–10	
1 Thessalonians 4:17	

Verse(s)	What This Passage Reveals to Me
Titus 2:11	
2 Peter 3:9	
John 3:16	
Revelation 13:8	
Romans 9:3	
Luke 13:24	

That was a big assignment! Ready for more? Okay, now select three favorite passages from this list and engage in the same study of those verses by using two different translations.

Translation #1: _____

Selected Verse(s)	What This Passage Reveals to Me

Translation #2: _____

Selected Verse(s)	What This Passage Reveals to Me

Act

We have covered a lot of ground in this study so far, so it might be a good time to pause and reflect on what you have learned. To accomplish this review in a more creative manner, imagine a scenario that finds you having coffee with a good friend who is skeptical to the afterlife, heaven, and hell. Because this person is your good friend, he or she has agreed to listen to you make a defense for those three topics. Using the space below, write out your presentation to your friend. It doesn't have to be long and deep, but it does need to be substantive. As you are gathering your thoughts, ask the Lord to give you the direction you need to go with each of these topics, especially in view of your friend's beliefs.

1. What would you say to your friend about your beliefs regarding the *afterlife*?

2. What would you say to your friend about your beliefs regarding *heaven*?

3. What would you say to your friend about your beliefs regarding *hell*?

4. What are three of the most significant discoveries you've made in these sessions?

5. What sort of difference will those discoveries make in the way you live your life?

Connect

It's time to contact your partner once again, either through text or phone call. Check in to see how he or she is doing. What did the person think about the content regarding hell? Is there any frustration or confusion he or she wants to verbalize? How do these truths about heaven and the afterlife make a difference in the way he or she is living? Is there anything you can do to be of help to this person? Talk to your partner about the answers to the previous questions—big truths you've come away with as a result of the study and how the time together has made a change in your life.

Reflect

Interview with Dr. Paul Copan

Dr. Paul Copan is a professor, has been a visiting scholar at Oxford University, and has served as president of the Evangelical Philosophical Society. His speaking ministry has taken him to countries around the world. Dr. Copan writes about hell in one of his most recent books, *Loving Wisdom: A Guide to Philosophy and Christian Faith.*

I asked Copan about the verses that talk about the destruction of the unredeemed. "As Bart Ehrman pointed out, Jesus said the broad gate leads to 'destruction' (see Matthew 7:13). On the surface, that sounds an awful lot like annihilation."

"Hold on a moment," Copan replied. "Destruction doesn't always mean cease to exist."

That seemed counterintuitive. "Really?" I asked. "Can you give an example?"

"Yes, 2 Peter 3:6 says that the world in Noah's day was destroyed. But we know it actually continued to endure. The same Greek word for *destroy—apollymi—*can be translated as 'lost,' as in the story about the lost—but existing—coin in Luke 15:9. Also, a 'second death' doesn't necessarily suggest being extinguished. After all, we were once dead in our trespasses and sins, though physically alive" (see Ephesians 2:1).

"What other passages argue against annihilationism?"

"There's 2 Thessalonians 1:9, which says the unrepentant will be 'punished with everlasting destruction and shut out from the presence of the Lord.' Why mention being excluded from God's presence if 'everlasting destruction' means they have totally perished? In contrast, 1 Thessalonians 4:17 says believers 'will be with the Lord forever.' Again, we see a parallel, indicating ongoing existence for both the redeemed and the unredeemed."

Copan went on to discuss several other New Testament passages that make more sense if hell involves eternal consciousness.

"Consider Judas. Jesus said in Mark 14:21 that it would have been better for him if he had not been born. That doesn't sound like Jesus is speaking of him moving from nonexistence to existence and then back into nonexistence again. The weightiness of Jesus' pronouncement is far more damning than that. Jesus has in mind more than simply Judas's permanent reputation of infamy.

"Jesus said it would be better to be maimed—without an eye or a hand—than to lose an intact sinning body by being thrown into hell (see Matthew 5:29–30) But if people simply cease to exist at some point after death, then this worry doesn't make sense. Interestingly, one scholar said that 'if hell is just lack of conscious existence, there would be a lot of situations in which people would find that to be more desirable than suffering as a maimed person in this life.'[1]

"Jesus says blasphemy against the Holy Spirit will not be forgiven, 'either in this age or in the age to come' (see Matthew 12:31–32). This suggests that those committing this sin would continue to exist in eternity.

"In John 3:36, Jesus says that whoever rejects the Son will not see life, for God's wrath abides on them. How does the wrath of God abide on someone who doesn't exist?

"Paul's use of the term 'everlasting destruction' (2 Thessalonians 1:9) is a specific reference to the intertestamental Jewish book 4 Maccabees, which is the only place this phrase is used in the relevant literature. And this book has several places that talk about conscious awareness in judgment—not annihilationism.[2]

"Annihilationists say the language of fire suggests the finality of existence. But it's curious that Jesus refers to the worm not dying and the fire not being quenched (see Mark 9:48). Why would he say that if he's just talking about a cessation of existence? Worms don't continue once something is consumed. Yes, fire is figurative language, but if a person ceases to exist, why emphasize that the fire does not go out?

"And if the unregenerate will also be raised bodily, though not in glory, why emphasize the image of 'immortal' worms continuing to feed on their body? Worms' unending feeding on a physical body in hell—a picture of torment—is far more severe than death or extinction itself. What's the big deal about a worm feeding on your body if you no longer exist? The same kind of language is found in the intertestamental book of Judith; there it refers to God's judgment in sending 'fire and worms into their flesh; they shall weep in pain forever.'[3] It appears that this final state of torment is worse than mere death itself. All of this suggests that something more than annihilationism is going on here."

—*From chapter 8 of* The Case for Heaven

For Next Week: Before your group's next session, read chapters 9–10 and the conclusion in *The Case for Heaven*.

How Do We Live with an Eye on Eternity?

• • • • • • • •

Since, then, you have been raised with Christ, set your hearts on things above, where Christ is, seated at the right hand of God. Set your minds on things above, not on earthly things.

Colossians 3:1–2

Welcome

Living with an eye on eternity. What comes to mind when you hear that phrase? What does living each day with an eye on eternity—on the life after this one—really look like? Perhaps no one better captures such a way of life than Joni Eareckson Tada.

If you don't know her story, Joni lived an active life growing up: she rode horses, hiked, played tennis, and swam. But then on July 20, 1967, she suffered an accident that changed her life. She dove into the Chesapeake Bay after misjudging the shallowness of the water, suffered a fracture in her vertebrae, and became paralyzed from the shoulders down.

In her autobiography, she described how the next two years of her life were filled with anger, depression, and doubts about her faith as she went through rehabilitation. But during this time, she also learned how to paint with a brush between her teeth. She even began selling some of her artwork. Now, decades later, she has written more than forty books, has starred in an auto-biographical movie about her life, and is an advocate for people with disabilities.

Joni truly epitomizes the phrase, *"getting my mind on the hereafter."* As she described in a recent interview, "Physical affliction and emotional pain are, frankly, part of my daily routine. But these hardships are God's way of helping me to get my mind on the hereafter. . . Stuck in a wheelchair and staring out the window at the fields of our farm, I wondered, *Lord, how in the world can you consider my troubles 'light and momentary'? I will never walk or run again. I've got a leaky leg bag. I smell like urine. My back aches. I'm trapped in front of this window.*

"Years later, however, the light dawned: The Spirit-inspired writers of the Bible simply had a different perspective, an end-of-time view. Nothing more radically altered the way I looked at my suffering than leapfrogging to this end-of-time vantage point. When God sent a broken neck my way, he blew out the lamps in my life that lit up the 'here and now' and made it so captivating. The dark despair of total and permanent paralysis that followed wasn't much fun, but it sure made heaven come alive."[1]

In this final session, we will examine how we can likewise gain this different perspective and end-of-time view that the Spirit-inspired writers of the Bible possessed.

Consider

Take some time to share at least one key takeaway or insight you had from last week's personal studies. Then, to get things started, pair up with another group member and briefly talk about the following questions:

- *Living with an eye on eternity.* What do you think is meant by that expression? Do you have any personal experience with this phrase?
- Who do you know who is suffering with some extreme circumstances? As you think about that person, how would Joni's words be meaningful to them?

Watch

Play the video segment for session five (see the streaming video access provided on the inside front cover). As you watch, use the following outline to record any thoughts or concepts that stand out to you.

When we live with a daily eye on heaven, it radically changes our attitude toward the difficulties we will inevitably face in this world.

Keeping an eye on heaven gives us a reminder of how much we are valued by God. The God of the universe, who could spend eternity any way he desires, wants to spend it with us.

Living with an awareness of heaven also puts our suffering into perspective. It gives us the courage we need to face the trials of life, knowing that heaven is waiting for us.

Living with the hope of heaven also fills us with the joy of anticipation. Our heavenly Father loves us and has created an environment custom-tailored to give us maximum enjoyment.

Heaven is a place where we will enjoy rich and deep relationships in the midst of a community that shares the common treasure of Christ. It is the home we have always longed for, where there is security, acceptance, love, and belonging, all custom designed for us.

Heaven is untainted by sin. It is a place where we will be comforted and made whole—a place beyond pain and disabilities.

Heaven will be a place where we will worship and serve God out of an overwhelming sense of awe, wonder, and love—and it will never get boring!

Two closing questions to consider: (1) Are you confident that you will spend eternity with God? (2) Who do you know in your life who doesn't have the assurance of heaven?

Discuss

Once the video has concluded, break up into small groups for a time of discussion. Once again, this should be the group with whom you've spent the previous sessions. Circle up and go for it!

1. **Read aloud 1 Peter 2:9.** What does this verse say about how God sees you and how much he values you? How can keeping an eye on heaven remind you of this truth?

2. **Read aloud Romans 8:18.** What does this verse say about your present trials? How can keeping an eye on heaven help you to endure through trying times?

3. **Read aloud 1 Corinthians 2:9.** What does this verse say about the place that God has prepared for his followers? How does this fill you with hope in this life?

4. What comes to mind when you picture the perfect home? What are some of the traits of that kind of home that you most want to experience in heaven?

5. Think about the final question posed at the end of this week's teaching: *Who do you know who doesn't have the assurance of heaven?* How would you respond to this question? What steps can you take to help that person have such assurance?

6. What is the most valuable discovery you've made during this study? What is something you did not know before this time together? Share it with the group.

Respond

Briefly review the outline for the session five teaching and any notes you took. In the space below, write down your most significant takeaway from this session.

Pray

As this session ends, spend some time together thanking the Lord for the blessings of these past five weeks. Hopefully, you've learned a lot, you've made some new friends, you've deepened some other relationships, and you've received a host of other advantages from being together.

Final Personal Study

Reflect on the content you have covered this final week by engaging in any or all of the following personal study. The time you invest will be well spent, so let God use it to draw you closer to him. Be sure to record any points or insights that stand out to you as you spent this time with the Lord.

Study

As this week's teaching came to a close, you were encouraged to "keep an eye on heaven as you go through your everyday life." One practical way to do this is to focus on passages from the Bible that speak about heaven. So, with this in mind, your challenge this week is to focus on ten such key passages—to read them, ponder them, pray about them, and record what they mean to you. After reading each of these passages, take a few minutes to write down an answer to the question, "What does this passage mean to me?" Some of these verses will be more meaningful to you than others—and that's okay. The goal is to just start developing a "heaven habit" that will tune your mind to think more about the hereafter.

Even though I walk through the darkest valley, I will fear no evil, for you are with me; your rod and your staff, they comfort me. You prepare a table before me in the presence of my enemies. You anoint my head with oil; my cup overflows. Surely your goodness and love will follow me all the days of my life, and I will dwell in the house of the LORD forever (Psalm 23:4–6).

"See, I will create new heavens and a new earth. The former things will not be remembered, nor will they come to mind" (Isaiah 65:17).

"For he is the living God and he endures forever; his kingdom will not be destroyed, his dominion will never end. He rescues and he saves; he performs signs and wonders in the heavens and on the earth" (Daniel 6:26–27).

"My Father's house has many rooms; if that were not so, would I have told you that I am going there to prepare a place for you? And if I go and prepare a place for you, I will come back and take you to be with me that you also may be where I am. You know the way to the place where I am going" (John 14:2–4).

I consider that our present sufferings are not worth comparing with the glory that will be revealed in us (Romans 8:18).

However, as it is written: "What no eye has seen, what no ear has heard, and what no human mind has conceived"—the things God has prepared for those who love him" (1 Corinthians 2:9).

Brothers and sisters, we do not want you to be uninformed about those who sleep in death, so that you do not grieve like the rest of mankind, who have no hope. For we believe that Jesus died and rose again, and so we believe that God will bring with Jesus those who have fallen asleep in him (1 Thessalonians 4:13–14).

I have fought the good fight, I have finished the race, I have kept the faith. Now there is in store for me the crown of righteousness, which the Lord, the righteous Judge, will award to me on that day—and not only to me, but also to all who have longed for his appearing (2 Timothy 4:7–8).

Then I saw "a new heaven and a new earth," for the first heaven and the first earth had passed away, and there was no longer any sea. I saw the Holy City, the new Jerusalem, coming down out of heaven from God, prepared as a bride beautifully dressed for her husband. And I heard a loud voice from the throne saying, "Look! God's dwelling place is now among the people, and he will dwell with them. They will be his people, and God himself will be with them and be their God. 'He will wipe every tear from their eyes. There will be no more death' or mourning or crying or pain, for the old order of things has passed away" (Revelation 21:1–4).

They will see his face, and his name will be on their foreheads. There will be no more night. They will not need the light of a lamp or the light of the sun, for the Lord God will give them light. And they will reign for ever and ever (Revelation 22:4–5).

Verse(s)	What This Passage Reveals to Me
Psalm 23:4–6	
Isaiah 65:17	
Daniel 6:26–27	
John 14:2–4	
Romans 8:18	
1 Corinthians 2:9	
1 Thessalonians 4:13–14	
2 Timothy 4:7–8	
Revelation 21:1–4	
Revelation 22:4–5	

Act

Use this final time to brainstorm how to use what you have learned during these past five sessions to reach out to others who don't know the message of the gospel. After all, knowing more about the afterlife, heaven, and hell is a real motivator to get the Word out to those who aren't aware of these truths. So, be sure to take a few minutes today to reflect on the following questions and then write your answers in the spaces provided.

1. During this week's group time, you considered the people in your life who do not have the assurance of heaven and how you can help them have that assurance. Now make this practical by writing down the names of four or five people in your immediate circle of family and friends who fall into this group.

2. Next, write out a short prayer for each of these people on your list. Ask God to give you an opportunity to share his plan of salvation with them and for other believers in Christ to also point them to the truth. Continue to pray for these people throughout the week.

3. Now comes the fun part! Next to each person's name, actually come up with a scenario that would provide a way to share the gospel message with them. The most effective way would be

to share with them your own personal testimony—how God changed your life through Christ and gave you assurance of eternal life in heaven. Your sharing could be by phone, text, email, but unquestionably the best way would be face to face.

4. Finally, write down your own prayer to God, asking him to give the courage and the opportunity to share your story of faith with those who need the assurance of heaven.

Connect

Make contact one last time with your partner by text or phone. Check in to see how he or she is doing. Did the person enjoy the study? Does he or she still have any frustration or confusion to verbalize? How do these truths about heaven and the afterlife make a difference in the way he or she is living? Is there anything you can do to be of help? Talk to your partner about the answers to the previous questions—big truths you've come away with as a result of the study and how the time together has made a change in your life.

Reflect

Interview with Luis Palau

The facts about Luis Palau are well known. He was only a youngster when his father died, plunging his family into poverty. But he rose to become "the Billy Graham of Latin America," an indefatigable evangelist whose ministry brought at least a million people into God's kingdom through the years. He influenced presidents and popes, spoke in seventy-five nations, had a radio program heard in Spanish and English on 4,200 stations, and wrote many books.

"If you could send back a message from heaven to your fellow Christians, what would it say?"

"To go for it," Palau said with vigor. "Take a risk—tell others about the good news of Christ. Remember that it's the job of the Holy Spirit to convict them of their sin. He's your partner—let him do his work in them. *You* bring them the best news on the planet—that there's redemption, there's a relationship with God, there's heaven, there's an eternal party that's waiting for them."

Palau recalled that when he was a new Christian, his mother would urge him to take the gospel to nearby towns that didn't have a church. "She kept encouraging me and pushing me," he said. "She'd say, 'Go, go, go. Get out and reach people with the good news!'"

"What did you say?" I asked.

"I was slow to step out in faith. I'd say to her, 'Mom, I'm waiting for the call.'" "I'm guessing she didn't respond well to that."

"No. She was getting upset. She said to me, 'The call? The *call*? The call went out two thousand years ago, Luis! The Lord's waiting for *your* answer! You're not waiting for *his* call!' And she was right. The Bible makes our task clear—go out and reach people with the gospel, whether they're friends, family members, neighbors, colleagues, or just people we meet along the path of life. That should be the default assignment for all of us. The absence of a specific call should never be an excuse for inaction."

"Did that get you moving?"

"It was one of the defining moments of my life," he answered. "I realized I didn't need to wait around; instead, I needed to *do*. And that's how I'd encourage my fellow believers—step out in faith, take action, strike up a conversation with someone far from God. Whether they accept the gospel is up to them. You can't control that. But I can tell you from personal experience that at the end of your life, when all is said and done, you'll never regret being courageous for Christ."

His comment made me think of the words of evangelist Becky Manley Pippert: "We are living after Jesus came from heaven to earth and before Jesus returns again to bring heaven to earth. What is the significance of God placing us here at this particular juncture in history? It is so that we can join God in his quest to love, seek, and invite people to come home to God!"[1]

"And what about people who aren't Christians?" I asked Palau. "What message would you send them from heaven?"

Palau didn't mince words. "I'd tell them, 'Don't be stupid!'"

We both burst out laughing. "Seriously?" I said. "That's *it*?"

"Sure—don't be stupid! Don't pass up what God is offering out of his love and grace. Why embrace evil when goodness beckons? Why turn your back on heaven and choose hell? Why expose yourself to the harmful side effects of a sinful life when you can follow God's path of righteousness and healing? Don't miss the party that God has waiting for you in heaven!"

Somehow, when I had gotten on the plane to fly to Oregon to meet with one of the world's most renowned evangelists, I didn't expect our interview to end with him simply saying, "Don't be stupid." Then again, that stark exhortation does sum up this study pretty well.

The evidence points to heaven being a reality. Jesus has flung open the gates for everyone who wants to enter through repentance and faith. Hope is waiting. Grace is calling. The party is starting. The admission is paid. Eternity is in the balance.

Seek God. Trust him. Follow him. Heed the words of my friend and hero Luis Palau. *"Don't be stupid!"*

—*From chapter 10 of* The Case for Heaven

Leader's Guide

Thank you for your willingness to lead your group through this study! What you have chosen to do is valuable and will make a great difference in the lives of others. The rewards of being a leader are different from those who are participating, and we hope that as you lead you will find your own walk with Jesus deepened by this experience.

The Case for Heaven is a five-session study built around video content and small-group interaction. As a group leader, think of yourself as the host. Your job is to take care of your guests by managing the behind-the-scenes details so that when everyone arrives, they can enjoy their time together. As the leader, your job is not to answer all the questions or reteach the content—the video, book, and study guide will do that work. Your job is to guide the experience and cultivate your small group into a kind of teaching community. This will make it a place for members to process, question, and reflect—not receive more instruction.

Before your first meeting, make sure everyone in the group gets a copy of the study guide. This will keep everyone on the same page and help the process run more smoothly. If some group members are unable to purchase the guide, arrange it so that people can share the resource with other group members. Giving everyone access to all the material will position this study to be as rewarding an experience as possible. Everyone should feel free to write in his or her study guide and bring it to group every week.

Setting Up the Group

You will need to determine with your group how long you want to meet each week so you can plan your time accordingly. Generally, most groups like to meet from one to two hours, so you could use one of the following schedules:

Section	60 min	90 min	120 min
INTRODUCTION (members arrive)	5 min	5 min	10 min
CONSIDER (discuss the icebreaker questions)	10 min	15 min	15 min
WATCH (watch the video teaching)	15 min	15 min	15 min
DISCUSS (discuss the group questions)	25 min	40 min	60 min
RESPOND & PRAY (close the group time)	5 min	15 min	20 min

As the group leader, you will want to create an environment that encourages sharing and learning. A church sanctuary or formal classroom may not be as ideal as a living room, because those locations can feel formal and less intimate. No matter what setting you choose, provide enough comfortable seating for everyone and, if possible, arrange the seats in a semi-circle so everyone can see the video easily. This will make transition between the video and the group conversation more efficient and natural.

Also, try to get to the meeting site early so you can greet participants as they arrive. Simple refreshments create a welcoming atmosphere and can be a wonderful addition to a group study evening. Try to take food and pet allergies into account to make your guests as comfortable as possible. You may also want to consider offering childcare for couples with children who want to attend. Finally, be sure your media technology is working properly. Managing these details up front will make the rest of your group experience flow smoothly and provide a welcoming space in which to engage the content of *The Case for Heaven*.

Starting the Group Time

Once everyone has arrived, it is time to begin the group. Here are some simple tips to make your group time healthy, enjoyable, and effective. Begin the meeting with a short prayer and remind the group members to put their phones on silent. This is a way to make sure you can all be present with one another and with God. Next, facilitate the "Before You Watch" icebreaker questions, using the directions provided in the study guide. This won't require as much time in session one, but beginning in session two, you may need more time if people also want to share any insights from their personal studies.

Leading the Discussion Time

Now that the group is engaged, watch the video and respond with some directed small-group discussion. Encourage the group members to participate in the discussion, but make sure they know they don't have to do so. As the discussion progresses, follow up with comments such as, "Tell me more about that," or "Why did you answer that way?" This will allow the group participants to deepen their reflections and invite meaningful sharing in a nonthreatening way.

Although there are only four discussion questions for each session, you do not have to use them all or even follow them in order. Feel free to pick and choose the questions based on either the needs of your group or how the conversation is flowing. Also, don't be afraid of silence. Offering a question and allowing up to thirty seconds of silence is okay. It allows people space to think about how they want to respond and also gives them time to do so.

As group leader, you are the boundary keeper for your group. Do not let anyone (yourself included) dominate the group time. Keep an eye out for group members who might be tempted to "attack" folks they disagree with or try to "fix" those having struggles. These kinds of behaviors can derail a group's momentum, so they need to be steered in a different direction. Model active listening and encourage everyone in your group to do the same. This will make your group time a safe space and create a positive community.

The group discussion leads to a closing time of reflection and prayer. During this time, encourage the participants to review what they have learned and share any needs they have with the group. Close your time by taking a few minutes to pray for those needs and to thank God for the reality of an afterlife and heaven. The group members may also want to share requests they want the other members to pray about during the week. Beginning in session two, be sure to check in regarding these requests and see how God has answered them.

At the end of each session, invite the group members to complete the between-sessions personal study for that week. If you so choose, explain you will provide some time before the video teaching next week for anyone to share insights. Let them know sharing is optional, and it's not a problem if they can't get to the between-sessions activities some weeks. It will still be beneficial for them to hear from the other participants and learn about what they discovered.

Thank you again for taking the time to lead your group. You are making a difference in the lives of others and having an impact on the kingdom of God.

Notes

Session 1

1. See Sharon Dirckx, *Am I Just My Brain?* (London: Good Book, 2019), 47–48. She attributes this thought experiment to Frank Jackson.
2. See Gottfried Wilhelm Leibniz, *Philosophical Papers and Letters,* 2nd ed. (Boston: Reidel, 1976).
3. Adrian Owen, "How Science Found a Way to Help Coma Patients Communicate," *The Guardian,* September 5, 2017, www .theguardian.com/news/2017/sep/05/how-science-found-a-way-to -help-coma-patient-communicate.
4. Wilder Penfield, *The Mystery of the Mind: A Critical Study of Consciousness and the Human Brain* (Princeton, NJ: Princeton University Press, 1975), 77–78.
5. See Dirckx, *Am I Just My Brain?* 69, 84.

Session 2

1. Louis Epstein, Robert Young, Miguel Quesada, et. al, "Table B – Verified Supercentenarians (Ranked by Age)," *Gerontology Research Group* (January 1, 2015). See also "List of the Verified Oldest People," wikipedia, https://en.wikipedia.org/wiki/List _of_the_verified_oldest_people#cite_note-GRG-B-2015-7.
2. "There Are Now More than Half a Million People Aged 100 or Older Around the World," *World Economic Forum,*

101

https://www.weforum.org/agenda/2021/02/living-to-one
-hundred-life-expectancy/.

3. "How Many People Live to 100?" *Genealogy InTime Magazine,*
http://www.genealogyintime.com/GenealogyResources/Articles
/how_many_people_live_to_100_page1.html

4. John Burke, *Imagine Heaven: Near- Death Experiences, God's
Promises, and the Exhilarating Future That Awaits You* (Grand
Rapids: Baker, 2015), back cover.

5. See R. C. Sproul, *Now, That's a Good Question!* (Wheaton, IL:
Tyndale, 1996), 300.

6. See J. P. Moreland and Gary R. Habermas, *Immortality: The Other
Side of Death* (Nashville: Nelson, 1992).

7. See Burke, *Imagine Heaven,* 51.

8. See Bonnie Malkin, "Girl Survives Sting by World's Deadliest
Jellyfish," *Telegraph,* April 26, 2010, www.telegraph.co.uk/news
/7638189 /Girl- survives- sting- by- worlds- deadliest- jellyfish
.html.

9. For a full report on Ian McCormack's experience, see Burke,
Imagine Heaven, 139–41.

Session 3

1. Charles R. Swindoll, *Swindoll's Living Insights New Testament
Commentary—Revelation* (Carol Stream, IL: Tyndale House,
2014), 298.

2. N. T. Wright, *Simply Good News: Why the Gospel Is News and What
Makes It Good* (San Francisco: HarperOne, 2015), 99, italics in
original.

3. See Bart D. Ehrman, *Heaven and Hell: A History of the Afterlife*
(New York: Simon & Schuster, 2020), xxi.

4. See Isaiah 25:6–10; 26:19; Hosea 6:1–2; Ezekiel 37; Daniel 12:2–3.
Scot McKnight said to me, "In God's providence and in the
unfolding of revelation and redemption, we only learn about a new
life beyond death in the final sections of the Old Testament, the
Prophets."

5. See Rodney Stark, *What Americans Really Believe: New Findings*

from the Baylor Study of Religion (Waco, TX: Baylor University
Press, 2008), 69–74.

6. Billings, *End of the Christian Life*, 151; see Maggie Fox, "Fewer
   Americans Believe in God— Yet They Still Believe in Afterlife,"
   Today, March 21, 2016, www.nbcnews.com/better/wellness/Fewer
   -americans-believe-god-yet-they-still-believe-afterlife-n542966.

7. See Fox, "Fewer Americans Believe in God."

8. C. S. Lewis, *The Weight of Glory* (1949; reprint, San Francisco:
   HarperSanFrancisco, 2001), 29, 32.

9. C. S. Lewis, *Mere Christianity* (1943; reprint, New York:
   Macmillan, 1960), 120.

10. Jerry Walls, *Heaven: The Logic of Eternal Joy* (New York: Oxford
    University Press, 2002), 31.

Session 4

1. Craig L. Blomberg, *Can We Still Believe in God? Answering Ten
   Contemporary Challenges to Christianity* (Grand Rapids: Brazos,
   2020), 29.

2. See 4 Maccabees 9:9; 10:10–11; 12:12, 18

3. Judith 16:17 (NRSV). This same fate of fire and worms is found
   in the intertestamental book of Sirach 7:17. Literal "immortal"
   worms continually feeding on literal bodies—drawn from Isaiah
   66:24 and Mark 9:48—appear in later literature such as the third
   - century Vision of Ezra (34) and the fourth- century Apocalypse
   of Paul (42).

Session 5

1. Joni Eareckson Tada, "Suffering Helps Me See Heaven,"
   Christianity Today, November 6, 2018, https://www.christianity
   today.com/ct/2018/november-web-only/joni-eareckson-tada
   -suffering-helps-me-see-heaven.html.

2. Rebecca Manley Pippert, *Stay Salt: The World Has Changed, Our
   Message Must Not* (Charlotte, NC: Good Book, 2020), 231.

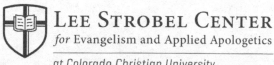

LEE STROBEL CENTER
for Evangelism and Applied Apologetics
at Colorado Christian University

Mark Mittelberg
Executive Director

Lee Strobel
Founding Director

Equipping Christians, ministry leaders, and churches to effectively share the grace of God and confidently defend the truth of the gospel, in order to reach our world for Christ.

Earn your accredited bachelor's or master's degree in Applied Apologetics with an emphasis in Innovative Evangelism—100% online!

Use promo code **CONTAGIOUSFAITH**
to waive the $50 application fee.

CCU also offers non-degree personal and spiritual growth courses at a reduced rate.

Learn more at *strobelcenter.com*

LIFE AFTER DEATH.

IT'S ONE OF HUMANKIND'S MOST PROVOCATIVE AND
OFTEN AVOIDED QUESTIONS...**UNTIL NOW.**

THE CASE FOR HEAVEN

New York Times best-selling author and journalist Lee Strobel
investigates the evidence for life after death in his new documentary.

ONLY IN THEATERS THIS SPRING

thecaseforheavenmovie.com

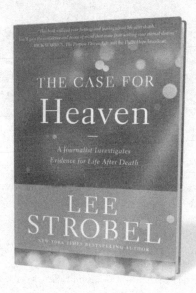

— ALSO AVAILABLE FROM LEE STROBEL —

Strobel investigates the story of Jesus' birth and resurrection and reveals how we can know that it actually took place.

The Case for Christmas and *The Case for Easter* are now available as studies for your church or small group.

These two studies (four weeks each) investigate the stories surrounding the birth and resurrection of Jesus—and how we can know that they are true.

The Case for Christmas/The Case for Easter DVD— Two studies in one! 9780310099314

The Case for Christmas Study Guide 9780310099291

The Case for Easter Study Guide 9780310099277

Available now at your favorite bookstore,
or streaming video on StudyGateway.com.

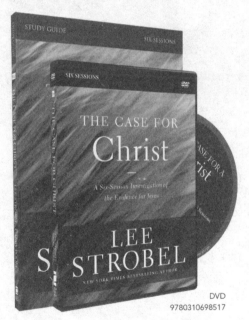

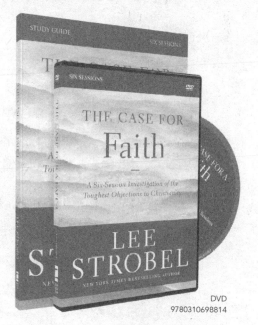

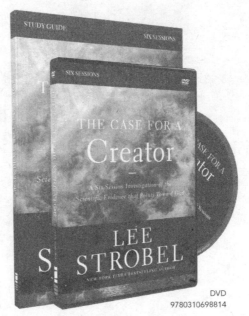

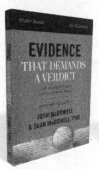